A Map of Your State

Use the map of the United States on page R8 of your social studies textbook to make a map of your own state.

Copy or trace the shape of your state onto a sheet of paper. Locate and label your state capital. Then add a compass rose. Color your map and give it a title. The title of your map could be the name of your state.

Macmillan/McGraw-Hill

Mystery State in the Northwest

Look at the map of the United States on page R8 of your social studies textbook. Use these clues to find the mystery state:

> The northeastern border of this state touches Montana. The capital of this state is about 450 miles east of the Pacific Ocean.

Write the name of the mystery state on a sheet of paper. Then make up clues for your own mystery state. Be sure to use direction words and distances in your clues.

Macmillan/McGraw-Hill

United States

A Trip to Nashville

Look at the map of the United States on page R8 of your social studies textbook.

Suppose you and your family want to take a trip from your state capital to Nashville, Tennessee. Which states would you pass through along the way? List the states in order on a sheet of paper. Next to each state write the name of its capital.

United States

Find the Cities

Use the map of the United States on page **R8** of your social studies textbook to find the following cities:

- **Reno, Nevada**
- **Springfield, Illinois**
- **New Orleans, Louisiana**

List the cities on a sheet of paper. Next to each city write the numbers of the lines of latitude and longitude that are closest to that city.

Macmillan/McGraw-Hill

United States

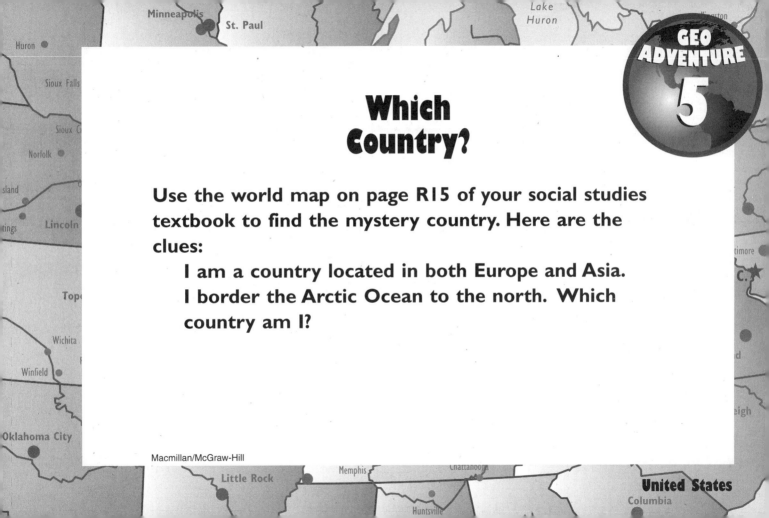

Which Country?

GEO ADVENTURE 5

Use the world map on page R15 of your social studies textbook to find the mystery country. Here are the clues:

I am a country located in both Europe and Asia. I border the Arctic Ocean to the north. Which country am I?

Macmillan/McGraw-Hill

Mystery City

Use the maps of the United States on pages R8 and R10 of your social studies textbook to find the mystery city. Here are the clues:

This city is a state capital. It is located near a large bay of the Atlantic Ocean. The bay does not border New Jersey.

Write the name of the mystery city and the bay on a sheet of paper.

Macmillan/McGraw-Hill

United States

About Alaska

Use the maps of the United States on pages R8 and R10 of your social studies textbook to answer these questions:

- Which bodies of water border Alaska?
- What is the capital of Alaska?
- About how many miles from the west coast of Alaska is Mt. McKinley?

Write the answers to these questions as a paragraph about Alaska.

Macmillan/McGraw-Hill

The Gulf of Mexico

Suppose you know a scientist who wants to study wildlife near the coast of the Gulf of Mexico. The scientist has asked you which of the United States he will have to visit in order to see all of the coastline near the gulf. Use the map of the United States on page R8 of your social studies textbook to help you figure out which states the scientist must visit. Make a list of the states. Next to each state, write the name of a city where the scientist might spend some time.

The Mountain Mystery State

Use the map of the United States on page R10 of your social studies textbook to find this mystery state:

This state is almost completely mountainous. It has more than 150 miles of coastline on the Atlantic Ocean.

Write the name of the mystery state on a sheet of paper. Then make up clues for another mystery state. Be sure to include clues about the landforms in the state.

Macmillan/McGraw-Hill

Latitude and Longitude

Turn to the maps of latitude and longitude on page G5 of your social studies textbook. Then copy these sentences:

- Lines of latitude measure the distance from the prime meridian.
- Lines of longitude are also called parallels.
- Latitude lines extend north and south.

If a sentence states something true, write *T* next to it. If a sentence is false, write *F* next to it. Rewrite each false sentence so it says something true.

Macmillan/McGraw-Hill

United States

Continent Chart

Use the world map on page R14 of your social studies textbook and the hemisphere maps on page G5 to make a chart of facts about the continents. The chart should include:

- the name of each continent
- the hemispheres in which each continent is located
- the name of one country on each continent

You can organize the information under the headings *Continent, Location,* and *Country.*

Macmillan/McGraw-Hill

Country Detective

Turn to the map of the Western Hemisphere on page R6 of your social studies textbook. Use these clues to find the mystery country:

This country is south of the equator and west of 60°W longitude. Its capital city is Lima.

Write the name of the mystery country on a sheet of paper. Then make up clues for another mystery country. Be sure to include latitude and longitude in your clues.

Macmillan/McGraw-Hill

United States

More Latitude and Longitude

Use the maps of latitude and longitude on page 40 of your social studies textbook to answer these questions:

- In which direction do lines of latitude extend?
- What do lines of latitude measure?
- In which direction do lines of longitude extend?
- Where do lines of longitude begin and end?

Write the answers to these questions as a paragraph about latitude and longitude.

Macmillan/McGraw-Hill

A Route in South America

Use the map of the **Western Hemisphere** on page **R6** of your social studies textbook to follow these directions:

Find the capital of Venezuela. Travel south from this city until you reach 30°S latitude. Follow 30°S latitude east until you reach the Atlantic Ocean. What city is located there?

Write the name of the city and the country. Then list all the countries you passed through along the way.

Macmillan/McGraw-Hill

Rapid City

prings

Dodge City

United States

Scottsdale

Tucson

Roswell

Chic

er

akland

Jose

Fres

Los An

icali

Your State: True or False?

Turn to the map of the United States on page R8 of your social studies textbook. Copy these sentences:

- **My state is west of the Mississippi River.**
- **My state is more than 300 miles from the 110°W meridian.**
- **My state is less than 600 miles from the border of Canada.**

If a sentence states something true about your state, write *T* next to it. If a sentence is false, write *F* next to it. Then rewrite each false statement to make it true.

Macmillan/McGraw-Hill

United States

Bordering the Pacific Ocean

Turn to the map of the Western Hemisphere on page R6 of your social studies textbook. Name two North American countries that border the Pacific Ocean and are completely east of 90°W longitude. Which South American countries border the Pacific Ocean and are completely south of the equator?

Finding Locations

Suppose you know someone who is learning how to make maps. Your friend needs help with a map of the Western Hemisphere. Use the map of the Western Hemisphere on page R6 of your social studies textbook to help you find these locations:

- 60°N latitude, 150°W longitude
- 30°N latitude, 120°W longitude
- 0° latitude, 60°W longitude

On a sheet of paper, write the name of the city that is located where the lines of latitude and longitude cross.

Macmillan/McGraw-Hill

Regions

Turn to the map of Regions of the United States on page 29 of your social studies textbook. Then answer the following questions:

- Of which region are Florida and Arkansas a part?
- Which states in the West region border the Southwest region?
- Which region extends farthest east?

Write the answers as sentences in a paragraph about regions of the United States.

Macmillan/McGraw-Hill

United States

Sailing Around the World

Use the world map on page R14 of your social studies textbook to plan a sailing trip around the world. Your trip must begin and end in Hawaii. You may not cross any land.

Write a description of the route you would take. Be sure to name the bodies of water you would cross and the directions in which you would travel.

Macmillan/McGraw-Hill

Map Scale: True or False?

Turn to the maps of Hawaii on page G7 of your social studies textbook. Then copy these sentences:

- The scales on both maps show only miles.
- On both maps the scales show that one inch equals 150 miles.
- On both maps the distance between Niihau and Oahu is about 130 miles.

If a sentence states something true, write *T* next to it. If a sentence is false, write *F* next to it. Then rewrite each false statement to make it true.

Macmillan/McGraw-Hill

Across the United States

Suppose you know someone who wants to travel across the United States from the coast of the Pacific Ocean to the coast of the Atlantic Ocean. To make sure she follows a straight route, your friend wants to follow the line of 40°N latitude. Use the map of the 50 United States on pages R12 and R13 to find which states your friend will cross. On a sheet of paper, list the states in order.

Macmillan/McGraw-Hill

Georgia and North Dakota

Use the map of the United States on page R8 of your social studies textbook to complete a chart.

	Georgia	North Dakota
borders an ocean		
is north of 40°N latitude		
is east of 90°W longitude		

Copy the chart onto a sheet of paper. Then put a check in the box next to each phrase that describes Georgia or North Dakota.

Macmillan/McGraw-Hill

United States

Native Americans

Turn to the map of Native Americans in the 1500s on page 76 of your social studies textbook. In which cultural area did the Inuit live? Which other Native Americans lived in the same area?

In which cultural area did the Cheyenne live? Which other cultural areas bordered that area?

Macmillan/McGraw-Hill

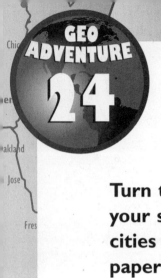

Cities Near 40°N Latitude

Turn to the map of the United States on page R8 of your social studies textbook. Find 40°N latitude. Which cities are near 40°N latitude? List them on a sheet of paper in order from west to east.

Macmillan/McGraw-Hill

United States

A Pennsylvania Road Map

Look at the road map of Pennsylvania on page G11 of your social studies textbook. Suppose you know someone who wants to travel from Allentown to Harrisburg. What route should your friend follow?

Suppose your friend wants to go to Johnstown after she visits Harrisburg. Write directions for your friend to follow.

Macmillan/McGraw-Hill

River Riddle

Use the map of the United States on page R10 of your social studies textbook to solve a river riddle.

I flow from the northeast to the southwest. My source is in the Rocky Mountains. I empty into the Gulf of California. Which river am I?

Macmillan/McGraw-Hill

United States

Mountains East and West

Look at the map of the United States on page R10 of your social studies textbook. Find as many mountain ranges as you can. List the names of the ranges on a sheet of paper. Write *west* next to mountain ranges that are west of 90°W longitude. Write *east* next to mountain ranges that are east of 90°W longitude.

Macmillan/McGraw-Hill

East of the Mississippi River

Turn to the physical map of the United States on page R10 of your social studies textbook. Find the part of the United States that is east of the Mississippi River. Write the words *northern, central,* and *southern* on a sheet of paper. Below each word, write the names of three landforms or physical features found in that part of the eastern United States.

Mystery States

Look at the map of the United States on page R8 of your social studies textbook. Use this clue to find the mystery states:

These states are crossed by 110°W longitude. Which four states could the mystery state be? Write the names on a sheet of paper. Then write one more clue that would narrow the mystery states from four to one mystery state.

Macmillan/McGraw-Hill

The Amazon River

Turn to the physical map of the **Western Hemisphere** on page **R7** of your social studies textbook. Then answer these questions about the Amazon River:

- In which mountain range is the source of the river?
- In which country is the mouth, or end, of the river?
- Into what body of water does the river empty?

Write the answers as sentences in a paragraph about the Amazon River.

Macmillan/McGraw-Hill

Your Own Mystery State

Use the map of the United States on page R8 of your social studies textbook to write clues that would help someone else find a mystery state. Choose a state to write about. Then write a sentence for each clue.

- Tell where the state is located.
- Name other states that are nearby.
- Name the state capital.

Macmillan/McGraw-Hill

United States

Using a Map Key

Look at the map of African Kingdoms on page 121 of your social studies textbook. Which of the following questions could you answer using the map key?

- How did people get from the Mediterranean Sea to Gao?
- Which was farther south—Kilwa or Mombasa?
- When did the Kongo kingdom begin?
- About how far from Zanzibar was Zimbabwe?

Elevation and Relief Maps

GEO ADVENTURE 33

Use the maps on page G10 of your social studies textbook to complete a chart.

	elevation	relief
shows changes in Earth's surface		
uses shading to show differences in land height		
shows land height above sea level		

Copy the chart onto a sheet of paper. Put a check in the box next to each phrase that describes the elevation map or the relief map.

Macmillan/McGraw-Hill

The Voyages of Columbus

Use the map showing the Voyages of Columbus on page 142 of your social studies textbook to finish this paragraph:

On his _____ voyage, Columbus sailed to _____ and met the Taino. Columbus sailed for the second time in _____. Nearly ten years later, Columbus began his _____ voyage. He sailed _____ of Hispaniola and _____, then reached the east coast of _____.

About How Far?

Turn to the map of the Western Hemisphere on page R6 of your social studies textbook. Find the capital of Peru. About how far from the capital of Peru is Rio de Janeiro, Brazil? About how far from Rio de Janeiro is the capital of Uruguay? Which city in Argentina is about 1,000 miles from the capital of Uruguay?

Macmillan/McGraw-Hill

The Ruined City

Suppose you found the journal of an explorer. One of the entries describes the location of a ruined city overgrown with plant life. Look at the map of the world on page R14 of your social studies textbook. Then read the clues and try to figure out where the city is.

> The city is west of 0° longitude. It is near the equator in a country that borders the Atlantic Ocean.

Where is the ruined city?

Macmillan/McGraw-Hill

A Pen Pal in North America

Suppose you received a letter from a pen pal in North America. In the letter your pen pal described his life along the coast of the Pacific Ocean. When you began to write back, you discovered that you had lost your pen pal's address.

Use the map of the Western Hemisphere on page R6 of your social studies textbook to find countries where your pen pal might live. Make a list of the countries. Next to each country, write the name of the national capital.

Macmillan/McGraw-Hill

GEO ADVENTURE 38

South America and the Equator

Find **South America** on the map of the **Western Hemisphere** on page **R6** of your social studies textbook. Then answer these questions:

- Which countries does the equator cross?
- Which countries in South America are entirely north of the equator?
- Which countries are entirely south of the equator?

Write the answers to these questions as sentences in a paragraph about **South America** and the equator.

Macmillan/McGraw-Hill

United States

From Guatemala to Colombia

Turn to the map of the world on page R14 of your social studies textbook. Suppose you know someone who wants to travel from Guatemala to Colombia. Which countries will your friend cross along the way? List the countries in order on a sheet of paper.

Macmillan/McGraw-Hill

Mountains of South America

Turn to the map of the Western Hemisphere on page R7 of your social studies textbook. Then answer the following questions:

- Which mountain range is found in South America?
- In which directions does it extend?
- How tall is Mt. Aconcagua?

Write the answers to these questions as sentences in a paragraph about the mountains of South America.

A Visit to the Southeast

Use the map of the Southeast on page 33 of your social studies textbook to finish this story:

Mrs. Ramos left _____, the capital of Virginia, and drove southwest to Montgomery, the capital of _____. Next she drove about _____ miles to New Orleans. Then she drove about 150 miles _____ to Jackson, Mississippi.

Copy the story onto a sheet of paper. Use a number, a direction word, the name of a state, or the name of a city to complete each sentence.

Macmillan/McGraw-Hill

Mt. Rainier

Turn to the physical map of the United States on page R10 of your social studies textbook. Find Mt. Rainier. Then copy these sentences:

- Mt. Rainier is the tallest mountain in the United States.
- Mt. Rainier is north of Mt. St. Helens.
- Mt. Rainier is about 300 miles from Canada.

If a sentence states something true, write *T* next to it. If a sentence is false, write *F* next to it. Rewrite each false sentence so it says something true.

Macmillan/McGraw-Hill

United States

An Historical Map: True or False?

Turn to the map of the 13 Colonies on page G11 of your social studies textbook. Then copy these sentences:

- The map shows the United States in the 1800s.
- Maine was part of the New Hampshire colony.
- There were two different groups of colonies in the 1800s.

If a sentence states something true about the map, write *T* next to it. If a sentence is false, write *F* next to it. Rewrite each false sentence to make it true.

Macmillan/McGraw-Hill

A 2,000-Mile Trip

Suppose you want to plan a family trip from the national capital of the United States to a city about 2,000 miles away. Use the map of the Western Hemisphere on page R6 of your social studies textbook to plan the trip.

Find a city about 2,000 miles from the national capital. Write the name of the city on a sheet of paper. Then list the cities or countries you would pass through on your way there.

Macmillan/McGraw-Hill

United States

Which Map?

Turn to the maps of the **Western Hemisphere** on pages
R6 and **R7** of your social studies textbook. On a sheet
of paper, write answers to these questions:
- **What is the national capital of Costa Rica?**
- **Which river flows from the Rocky Mountains to the Hudson Bay?**
- **Which city is farther north—Rio de Janeiro or Brasília?**

Tell which map helped you answer each question.

Macmillan/McGraw-Hill

Following Rivers

Use the map of the United States on page R8 of your social studies textbook to help you follow these directions:

Find a city in Idaho that is not the state capital. Follow the river that is north of the city as it flows toward the Pacific Ocean until you come to the Columbia River. Follow the Columbia River west. What is the first city you reach?

United States

A State Fact Sheet

Turn to the map of the United States on page R8 of your social studies textbook. Find Indiana. Then write the following information in sentences on a fact sheet about Indiana:

- Use latitude and longitude to describe the location of the state.
- List the states or bodies of water that border the state.
- Name the state capital.
- Name other cities in the state.

Macmillan/McGraw-Hill

United States

The Tropic of Capricorn

Look at the map of the world on page R14 of your social studies textbook. Suppose you know someone who is planning a trip around the world that will begin and end in Australia. Your friend plans to follow the Tropic of Capricorn. Which countries will your friend cross?

Macmillan/McGraw-Hill

Mexico: True or False?

Turn to the map of the Western Hemisphere on page R6 of your social studies textbook. Then copy these sentences:

- Most of Mexico is north of 30°N latitude.
- Mexico borders the Pacific Ocean and Cuba.
- Most of Mexico is located between 90°W longitude and 120°W longitude.

If a sentence states something true about Mexico, write *T* next to it. If a sentence is false, write *F* next to it. Rewrite each false sentence to make it true.

Macmillan/McGraw-Hill

Claimed by the French

Look at the map showing the **Search for a Northwest Passage** on page 176 of your social studies textbook. Suppose you found the journal of a person who lived in an area claimed by the French after 1605. Where might the journal writer have lived? Which explorer might have claimed the area?

Macmillan/McGraw-Hill

United States

Where Are You?

Use the map of the world on page R14 of your social studies textbook to help you follow this route:

Begin in the country that borders the United States to the south. Go east in a straight line to a country in Africa that borders Tunisia and Mali. Then go northeast to a country that borders Mongolia and is partly in Europe. Where are you?

Macmillan/McGraw-Hill

Mystery Hemisphere

Use the map of the hemispheres on page **G5** of your social studies textbook and the world map on page **R14** to find the mystery hemisphere.

This hemisphere includes the countries of South Africa, Peru, and Australia. It does not include Canada or China. Which hemisphere is it?

Write the name of the hemisphere on a sheet of paper. Then make up clues for your own mystery hemisphere. Include the names of countries in your clues.

Macmillan/McGraw-Hill

United States

A Captain in the Caribbean

Turn to the map of the world on page R14 of your social studies textbook. Suppose you know the captain of a ship. The captain wants to travel from the tip of Florida to Martinique, and then to Aruba. After visiting Aruba, the captain wants to head back to Florida. What route might the captain take to get from place to place? Write directions so that another captain could follow the same route.

Macmillan/McGraw-Hill

Mystery States

Use the maps of the United States on pages R8 and R10 of your social studies textbook to find two mystery states.

These states are crossed by the Appalachian Mountains on the east. Their western border is formed by the Mississippi River.

Write the names of the mystery states on a sheet of paper. Then make up a clue that would narrow the mystery states from two to one state.

Macmillan/McGraw-Hill

United States

From Mexico City to Brasília

Find Mexico City on the map of the Western Hemisphere on page **R6** of your social studies textbook. Suppose a group of travelers wants to go from Mexico City, Mexico, to Brasília, Brazil.

- In what direction should the group travel?
- How many miles will the group travel?
- Which countries will the group pass through along the way?

Macmillan/McGraw-Hill

From Philadelphia to Erie

Use the road map of Pennsylvania on page G11 of your social studies textbook to plan a family trip. Suppose your family wants to travel from Philadelphia to Erie. What are two routes your family can take? Write directions for each route. Be sure to use direction words. Then write a sentence that explains which of the two routes you think your family should take and why.

Macmillan/McGraw-Hill

United States

Start in Florida

Use the map of the United States on page R8 of your social studies textbook to follow these directions:

Start at the state capital of Florida. Travel northeast for about 300 miles until you come to a capital city. Then travel north about 450 miles to a city in Pennsylvania. Which three cities have you visited?

Now write directions for someone else to follow. Be sure to use direction words and to include the number of miles to travel.

Macmillan/McGraw-Hill

Different Maps

Use the maps of the Western Hemisphere on pages R6 and R7 of your social studies textbook to complete a chart.

	political	physical
shows the location of cities		
shows land height		
has a map scale		

Copy the chart onto a sheet of paper. Put a check in the box next to each phrase that describes the political map or the physical map.

Macmillan/McGraw-Hill

United States

Find the Cities

Use the map of the **Western Hemisphere** on page **R6** of your social studies textbook to find the following cities:
- **Manaus, Brazil**
- **Rosario, Argentina**
- **Anchorage, Alaska**

List the cities on a sheet of paper. Next to each city, write the lines of latitude and longitude that are closest to that city.

Macmillan/McGraw-Hill

New England Colonies

Use the map of the New England Colonies on page 205 of your social studies textbook to answer the following questions:

- In what year was New Hampshire founded?
- In which colony was Hartford located?
- Which colony was founded first?

Write the answers as sentences in a paragraph about the New England colonies.

United States

Your Friend's Trip

Suppose you have a friend who is traveling from Guayaquil, Ecuador, to Comodora Rivadavia, Argentina. Use the map of the Western Hemisphere on page R6 of your social studies textbook to describe your friend's trip.

- Which cities and countries is your friend passing through?
- How many miles will your friend have traveled when she reaches Comodora Rivadavia?

Macmillan/McGraw-Hill

A Pen Pal in South America

Suppose you received a letter from a pen pal in South America. In the letter your pen pal described his home in a town near the border of Chile. When you began to write back, you discovered that you had lost your pen pal's address.

Use the map of the Western Hemisphere on page R6 of your social studies textbook to find countries where your pen pal might live. Make a list of the countries.

Macmillan/McGraw-Hill

The Geography of Utah

Find **Utah** on the map of the United States on page R10 of your social studies textbook. Then copy these sentences:

- **The Teton Range crosses Utah from north to south.**
- **The Great Salt Lake is in southeastern Utah.**
- **The Great Salt Lake Desert is west of the mountains in Utah.**

If a sentence states something true about Utah, write *T* next to it. If a sentence is false, write *F* next to it. Then rewrite each false statement to make it true.

Farther from New York City

Find New York City on the map of the United States on page R8 of your social studies textbook. Then use the map scale to answer this question:

Which city is farther from New York City—Pittsburgh, Pennsylvania, or Providence, Rhode Island?

Write the answer on a sheet of paper. Then write a sentence that gives the distance between New York City and each of the other cities.

Macmillan/McGraw-Hill

United States

The Middle Colonies

Use the map of the Middle Colonies on page 212 of your social studies textbook to answer the following questions:

- In which colony was Trenton located?
- In what year was Delaware founded?
- Which colonies bordered the Atlantic Ocean?

Write the answers as sentences in a paragraph about the Middle colonies.

Macmillan/McGraw-Hill

GEO ADVENTURE 66

A California Fact Sheet

Find California on the map of the United States on page R10 of your social studies textbook. Then answer these questions:

- What kinds of landforms are found in California?
- Which deserts are found in California?
- Which bodies of water border California or are located within the state?

Write the answers to these questions as sentences on a fact sheet about the geography of California. Be sure to write in complete sentences.

Macmillan/McGraw-Hill

United States

GEO
ADVENTURE
67

Comparing Continents

Use the physical map of the **Western Hemisphere** on page **R7** of your social studies textbook to complete a chart.

	North America	South America
is completely east of 90°W		
is crossed by the equator		
has mountains in the west		

Copy the chart. Then put a check in the box next to each phrase that describes **North America** or **South America**.

Macmillan/McGraw-Hill

Mystery Country

Use the map of the Western Hemisphere on page R6 of your social studies textbook to find the mystery country.

60°W longitude and 30°S latitude cross in this country.

Write the name of the country on a sheet of paper. Then write a clue for your own mystery country. Be sure to use latitude and longitude in the clue.

Macmillan/McGraw-Hill

120°E Longitude

Look at the map of the world on page R14 of your social studies textbook. Find 120°E longitude. Where does this line of longitude meet the equator? Where does 120°E longitude meet the Arctic Circle?

Macmillan/McGraw-Hill

GEO
ADVENTURE
70

From Santa Fe to Los Angeles

Use the maps of the United States on pages R8 and
R10 of your social studies textbook to finish this story:

Jan and her family left Santa Fe, New Mexico, and
drove west toward Arizona, crossing the _____ River.
At the border of Arizona and California, they
crossed the _____ River. Then they drove across the
_____ Desert before reaching Los Angeles.

Copy the story onto a sheet of paper. Write the name
of a physical feature to complete each sentence.

Macmillan/McGraw-Hill

United States

Europe:
True or False?

Turn to the map of the world on page R14 of your
social studies textbook. Then copy these sentences:
- Sweden is northwest of Poland.
- The United Kingdom is south of France.
- Spain, France, Italy, and Greece border the
  Mediterranean Sea.

If a sentence states something true about Europe,
write *T* next to it. If a sentence is false, write *F* next to
it. Rewrite each false sentence so it says something
true about Europe.

Macmillan/McGraw-Hill

Where Is Poland?

Look at the map of the world on page R14 of your social studies textbook. Find Poland. Write three sentences describing the country's location. In one of the sentences, tell which countries border Poland.

United States

A Trip to Chile

Find Bogotá, Colombia, on the map of the Western Hemisphere on page R6 of your social studies textbook. Suppose a group of travelers want to go from Bogotá to Santiago, Chile.

- In what direction should the group travel?
- Between which lines of longitude will the group travel?
- Which countries will the group pass through along the way?

Macmillan/McGraw-Hill

A River in South America

Use the map of the Western Hemisphere on page R6 of your social studies textbook to answer these questions:

- What is the largest river system in South America?
- Where is the source of the river?
- Where is its mouth, or end?
- Which countries does the river flow through?

Write the answers to these questions as sentences in a paragraph about the river in South America.

Macmillan/McGraw-Hill

Mystery Traveler

Use the map of the United States on page R8 of your social studies textbook to find the mystery traveler.

The mystery traveler is in a city very near 80°W longitude. In which three cities could she be? Write the names of the cities on a sheet of paper.

Then write one more clue that would narrow the cities from two to one city.

Macmillan/McGraw-Hill

A Visit to South America

Look at the map of the Western Hemisphere on page R6 of your social studies textbook. Suppose you know someone who wants to travel from the capital of Brazil to the capital of Peru and then to the capital of Paraguay. What route should the person take to get from city to city?

Write directions so that someone else could follow the same route. Be sure to include direction words and the number of miles between cities.

Macmillan/McGraw-Hill

United States

Down the Arkansas River

Suppose your family took a rafting trip down the Arkansas River. Use the map of the United States on page R8 of your social studies textbook to describe the trip.

Where is the source of the river? Through which states does the river flow? About how many miles long is it? Write the answers as sentences in a paragraph about your family trip.

Macmillan/McGraw-Hill

Mystery State

Turn to the map of the United States on page R8 of your social studies textbook. Use these clues to find the mystery state:

This state is bordered on the southwest by Georgia.

One of its cities is located near 80°W longitude.

Write the name of the mystery state on a sheet of paper. Then make up clues for your own mystery state. Include directions and latitude or longitude in your clues.

Macmillan/McGraw-Hill

United States

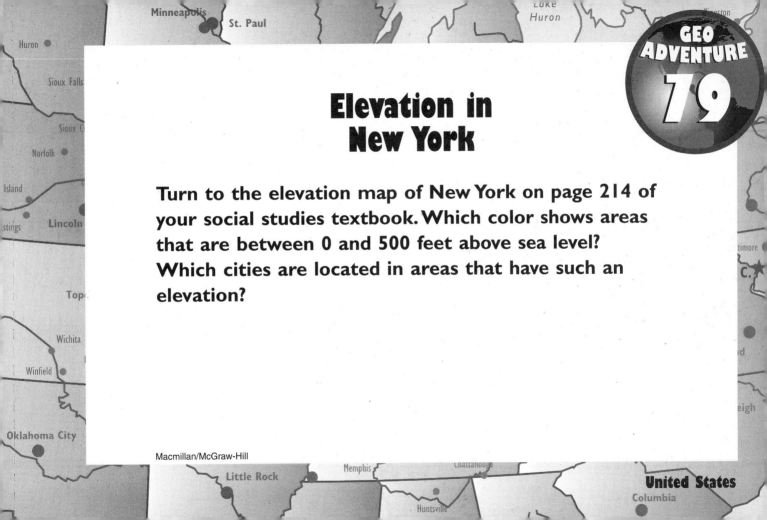

Elevation in New York

Turn to the elevation map of New York on page 214 of your social studies textbook. Which color shows areas that are between 0 and 500 feet above sea level? Which cities are located in areas that have such an elevation?

Macmillan/McGraw-Hill

Which Country?

Use the map of the Western Hemisphere on page **R6** of your social studies textbook to find the mystery country.

    This country is crossed by 120°W longitude and 60°N latitude. Which country is it?

Write clues for your own mystery country. Be sure to use latitude and longitude in one of your clues.

United States

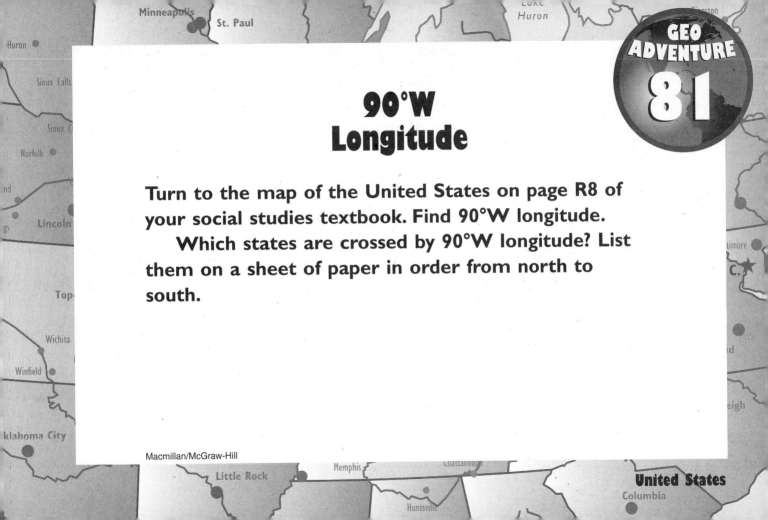

90°W
Longitude

Turn to the map of the United States on page R8 of your social studies textbook. Find 90°W longitude.

Which states are crossed by 90°W longitude? List them on a sheet of paper in order from north to south.

Macmillan/McGraw-Hill

United States

Finding Elevation and Relief

Turn to the elevation and relief maps of Washington on page G10 of your social studies textbook. Find the following cities:

- Spokane
- Seattle
- Olympia
- Yakima

List the cities on a sheet of paper. Next to each city, write whether it is located in an area of high, moderate, or low relief.

A Pen Pal in Africa

Suppose you received a letter from a pen pal in Africa. In the letter your pen pal described her home in a town near the coast of the Indian Ocean. When you began to write back, you discovered that you had lost your pen pal's address.

Use the map of the world on page R14 of your social studies textbook to find countries where you pen pal might live. Make a list of the countries.

Macmillan/McGraw-Hill

Mystery Hemisphere

Use the map of the hemispheres on page G5 of your social studies textbook and the world map on page R14 to find the mystery hemisphere.

This hemisphere includes the countries of France, India, and Ethiopia. It does not include the United States or Argentina. Which hemisphere is it?

Write the name of the hemisphere on a sheet of paper. Then make up clues for your own mystery hemisphere. Include the names of countries in your clues.

Find the Country

Turn to the world map on page R14 of your social studies textbook. Use the lines of latitude and longitude to find the locations listed below:

- 20°S latitude, 140°E longitude
- 60°N latitude, 140°E longitude
- 60°N latitude, 40°E longitude
- 0° latitude, 40°E longitude

On a sheet of paper, write the name of the country at each location.

Macmillan/McGraw-Hill

Mystery Country

Use the map of the world on page R14 of your social studies textbook to find the mystery country.

This country is a part of a peninsula. It is bordered by Portugal on the west and France on the northeast. Which country is it?

Write the name of the country on a sheet of paper. Then write clues for your own mystery country. Be sure to use geographic terms in your clues.

Macmillan/McGraw-Hill

A Great
Lakes Vacation

Suppose you know a group of people who are planning a vacation. The people want to visit a state where they will be able to spend time at the shore of one of the Great Lakes. Use the map of the United States on page R8 of your social studies textbook to help you figure out which states the people might visit. Make a list of the states. Next to each state, write the name of the capital city.

Macmillan/McGraw-Hill

Mystery States with a Desert

Turn to the map of the United States on page R10 of your social studies textbook. Use this clue to find the mystery states:

The Sonora Desert is in the southern part of these states.

Which two states could the mystery states be? Write both names on a sheet of paper. Then write a clue that narrows the mystery states down to one state.

Macmillan/McGraw-Hill

United States

A Trip from Bogotá, Colombia

Use the map of the Western Hemisphere on page R6 of your social studies textbook to finish this story:

> **Mr. Luna left Bogotá, Colombia, and went _____ to Santiago, Chile. Then he went _____ to Asunción, Paraguay. From Asunción he traveled _____ to La Paz, Bolivia. Finally, he flew _____ to Quito, Ecuador.**

Copy the story onto a sheet of paper. Use a direction word to complete each sentence.

Macmillan/McGraw-Hill

Mystery Countries

Use the map of the **Western Hemisphere** on page **R6** of your social studies textbook to find the mystery countries.

These countries are crossed by the equator. Which three countries could they be?

Write the names of the countries on a sheet of paper. Then write another clue to narrow the mystery countries from three to one country.

Which Capital City?

Turn to the maps of the United States on pages R8 and R10 of your social studies textbook. Find the state capitals of North Dakota, Maine, and New Mexico.

- Which capital city is close to both mountains and a river?
- What is the name of the mountain range?
- What is the name of the river?

Write the answers to these questions as sentences in a paragraph about the state capital.

Macmillan/McGraw-Hill

United States

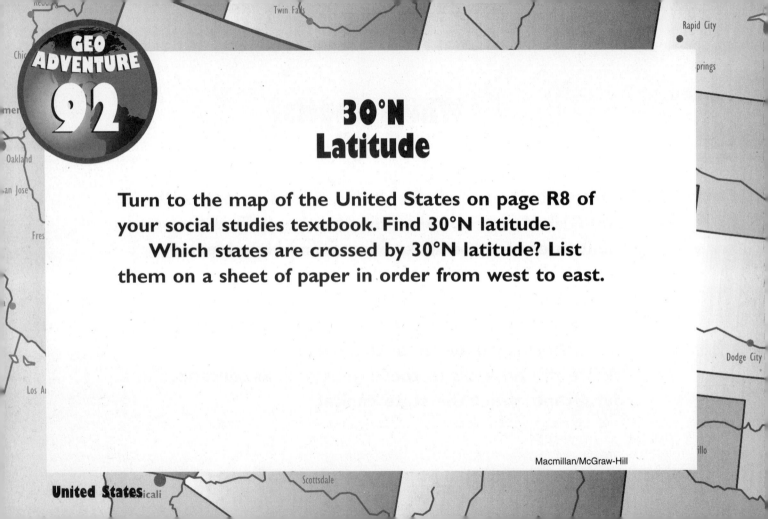

30°N
Latitude

Turn to the map of the United States on page **R8** of your social studies textbook. Find 30°N latitude.

Which states are crossed by 30°N latitude? List them on a sheet of paper in order from west to east.

Macmillan/McGraw-Hill

United States

The Battle of Yorktown

Look at the map showing the Battle of Yorktown on page 337 of your social studies textbook. Which of the following questions can you answer using the map key?

- Which cities are south of the James River?
- Which fleet was located near Cape Charles?
- About how far from Yorktown is Jamestown?
- Which forces surrounded Yorktown?
- Which rivers flow into Chesapeake Bay?

Macmillan/McGraw-Hill

Indiana's Corn and Dairy Farms

Look at the map of Indiana's Corn and Dairy Farms on page G8 of your social studies textbook. Then answer these questions:

- Where in Indiana is the Dairy-farming area?
- Where in Indiana is the Corn-growing area?
- If you lived near Ft. Wayne, which type of farms would you see?

Use the answers to these questions to write a fact sheet about corn and dairy farms in Indiana.

Macmillan/McGraw-Hill

United States

Land Near the Lakes

Turn to the elevation map of New York on page 214 of your social studies textbook. What is the elevation of land bordering Lake Ontario to the south? Is the land bordering Lake Erie higher or lower than the land near Lake Ontario? Explain how you figured out the answer.

Macmillan/McGraw-Hill

GEO
ADVENTURE
96

Mystery Traveler on Vacation

Use the inset map of Central America and the West Indies on page R14 of your social studies textbook to find the mystery traveler.

The mystery traveler is taking a vacation on an island in the Caribbean Sea. This island is east of 60°W longitude. On which island is he?

Macmillan/McGraw-Hill

Closer to Salt Lake City

Find Salt Lake City, Utah, on the map of the United States on page R8 of your social studies textbook. Then use the map scale to answer this question:

Which city is closer to Salt Lake City—Carson City, Nevada, or Boise, Idaho?

Write the answer on a sheet of paper. Then write sentences that tell the distances between Salt Lake City and the other cities.

Macmillan/McGraw-Hill

United States

The American Revolution

Turn to the historical map showing **Battles of the American Revolution** on page 332 of your social studies textbook. Then answer the following questions:

- In which state did the battle at Camden take place?
- In what year was the battle at Saratoga fought?
- In which states did battles take place in 1775?

Write the answers as sentences in a paragraph about the battles of the American Revolution.

Macmillan/McGraw-Hill

A Canada Fact Sheet

Look at the maps of the Western Hemisphere on pages R6 and R7 of your social studies textbook. Find Canada. Then answer the following questions:

- In what part of Canada are the Coast Mountains located?
- What is the national capital of Canada?
- Which lakes are located north of the Saskatchewan River?

Write the answers as sentences on a fact sheet about Canada.

Macmillan/McGraw-Hill

80°W
Longitude

Turn to the map of the world on page R14 of your social studies textbook. Find 80°W longitude.

Which countries are crossed by 80°W longitude? List them on a sheet of paper in order from north to south.

Macmillan/McGraw-Hill

United States

The Northwest Territory

Look at the map of the Northwest Territory on page 344 of your social studies textbook. Which states were formed from the Northwest Territory? Which country had claimed land west of the Mississippi River? Which country had claimed land north of the river?

Macmillan/McGraw-Hill

A Drive from Lansing, Michigan

Use the map of the United States on page R8 of your social studies textbook to finish this story:

Tim and his family left their home in Lansing, Michigan, and drove _____ for _____ miles to Norfolk, Virginia. From there they drove _____ for _____ miles to Charlotte, North Carolina. Then they drove _____ for _____ miles to Philadelphia, Pennsylvania.

Copy the story onto a sheet of paper. Use a direction word and the mileage traveled to complete each sentence.

Macmillan/McGraw-Hill

United States

Time Zones:
True or False?

Turn to the time zone map on page 522 of your social studies textbook. Then copy these sentences:
- A time zone is one of the six divisions of Earth used for measuring standard time.
- The time in any zone east of you is later than in your time zone.
- If it is 4:00 P.M. in New York City, it is 3:00 P.M. in Los Angeles.

If a statement is true, write *T* next to it. Then rewrite each false statement to make it true.

Macmillan/McGraw-Hill

United States

Mystery Hemisphere

Use the map of the hemispheres on page **G5** of your social studies textbook and the world map on page **R14** to find the mystery hemisphere.

This hemisphere includes the countries of Canada, Iran, and Japan. It does not include Argentina or Angola. Which hemisphere is it?

Make up clues for your own mystery hemisphere. Include the names of countries in your clues.

United States

Farther from Philadelphia

Find Philadelphia on the road map of Pennsylvania on page G11 of your social studies textbook. Then use the map scale to answer this question:

Which city is farther from Philadelphia—Pottstown or Lancaster?

Write the answer on a sheet of paper. Then write a sentence that tells the distance between Philadelphia and each of the other cities.

Macmillan/McGraw-Hill

The Lewis and Clark Expedition

Turn to the map of the Louisiana Purchase on page 381 of your social studies textbook. Find the route of the Lewis and Clark Expedition. Then answer these questions:

- Where did the expedition begin and end?
- Which mountains did it cross?
- Through which land areas did the expedition travel?

Write the answers as sentences in a paragraph about the Lewis and Clark Expedition.

United States

Visiting the Middle West

Turn to the map of the United States on page R8 of your social studies textbook. Suppose you have a friend who wants to travel from Gary, Indiana, to Wichita, Kansas. In which direction should your friend travel? About how many miles will she have to go?

After visiting Wichita, your friend wants to travel to a city about 150 miles away. To which cities might she go?

Macmillan/McGraw-Hill

A Mediterranean Cruise

Look at the inset map of Europe on page R15 of your social studies textbook. Find Gibraltar near the southern coast of Spain. Suppose you were taking a boat trip from Gibraltar to Sicily and then to Crete. What route would you take to get from place to place? About how many miles would you travel?

Macmillan/McGraw-Hill

North from South America

Turn to the map of the Western Hemisphere on page R6 of your social studies textbook. Find the southern tip of South America. Suppose a friend is traveling north in a straight line from Puenta Arenas, Chile, to the Arctic Ocean. Which countries will your friend pass through? Which bodies of water will she cross?

List the countries and bodies of water in order from south to north.

Mystery Traveler

Use the map of the United States on page R8 of your
social studies textbook to find the mystery traveler.
   The mystery traveler is in a city just west of 100°W
   longitude in a state that borders Canada. Where is
   she?

United States

What Time Is It?

Turn to the time zone map on page 522 of your social studies textbook. Find the time zone where you live. Suppose you are planning to make phone calls to friends in Chicago and Los Angeles. What time is it in Chicago right now? What time is it in Los Angeles?

Write your answers as complete sentences. Then explain how you know the time in these different cities.

Macmillan/McGraw-Hill

Cities in
South America

Turn to the map of the Western Hemisphere on page R6 of your social studies textbook. Find the capitals of Chile, Argentina, and Guyana.

Write the name of each city on a sheet of paper. Next to each city, write a description of its location using latitude and longitude.

A Trail to the West

Turn to the map of trails to the West on page 431 of your social studies textbook. Suppose you found the journal of someone who traveled with a group of people from Independence to Salt Lake City. Which trail might the people have followed? Which fort might they have passed along the way? What other things might the people have seen?

Macmillan/McGraw-Hill

States That Left the Union

Look at the map of the Union and the Confederacy on page 474 of your social studies textbook. Which slave states that left the Union bordered states that stayed in the Union? Which slave state that left the Union bordered territories?

Macmillan/McGraw-Hill

United States

Elevation and Relief

Turn to the elevation and relief maps on page G10 of
your social studies textbook. Then copy these
sentences:
- Both maps show the location of mountain ranges.
- The relief map shows the height above sea level of
  the Columbia Plateau.
- The relief map shows that Olympia has low relief.

If a sentence states something true, write *T* next to it.
If a sentence is false, write *F* next to it. Rewrite each
false statement to make it true.

Macmillan/McGraw-Hill

United States

Railroads in the West

Look at the map of Railroads in the West on page 515 of your social studies textbook. Suppose a family in Chicago in 1890 took a train to Seattle. On which railroad would they have traveled?

Suppose another family traveled from Kansas City to Los Angeles. Describe their trip.

Macmillan/McGraw-Hill

United States

Wisconsin and Arkansas

Use the map of the United States on page R8 of your social studies textbook and the time zone map on page 522 to complete the chart.

	Wisconsin	Arkansas
is in the Central Time Zone		
is crossed by 90°W longitude		
is north of 40°N latitude		

Copy the chart onto a sheet of paper. Put a check in the box next to each phrase that describes Wisconsin or Arkansas.

Macmillan/McGraw-Hill

Latitude and Longitude

Turn to the world map on page R14 of your social studies textbook. Use the lines of latitude and longitude to find the following locations:

- 40°N latitude, 100°W longitude
- 40°N latitude, 140°E longitude
- 20°S latitude, 20°E longitude
- 0° latitude, 20°E longitude

On a sheet of paper, write the name of the country at each location.

Macmillan/McGraw-Hill

United States

A Trip from Denver

Look at the map of the United States on page R8 of your social studies textbook and the time zone map on page 522. Suppose you have a friend who wants to travel from Denver to Pocatello, Idaho. From Pocatello, she wants to go to Seattle, Washington.

Which states and time zones will your friend pass through along the way? How many miles will she travel between each city?

Macmillan/McGraw-Hill

Mystery Traveler in Pennsylvania

Use the road map of Pennsylvania on page G11 of your social studies textbook to find out which cities the mystery traveler visited.

   The mystery traveler started at a city on Lake Erie. She drove south on Interstate 79 until it crossed Interstate 80. Then she drove east on Interstate 80 until she reached state highway 219. She traveled south on that highway about 60 miles.

On a sheet of paper, write the names of the cities where the mystery traveler started and ended her trip.

Macmillan/McGraw-Hill

Which Distance Is Shorter?

Use the map of the Western Hemisphere on page R6 of your social studies textbook to answer this question:
> Which distance is shorter?
> From La Paz, Bolivia, to Santiago, Chile?
> From Mexico City, Mexico, to New York City?

Write the answer on a sheet of paper. Then write a sentence that tells the number of miles between the two cities in each pair.

Macmillan/McGraw-Hill

GEO
ADVENTURE
122

Mystery Traveler Code

Turn to the map of the United States on page R8 of your social studies textbook. Suppose the mystery traveler gave you this coded message about a trip he was planning:

> I'm going to 40°N latitude, 110°W longitude; then to 30°N latitude, 100°W longitude; and then to 40°N latitude, 80°W longitude.

Which states does the mystery traveler plan to visit?

Macmillan/McGraw-Hill

Using a Map Key

Turn to the map of Indiana's Corn and Dairy Farms on page G8 of your social studies textbook. Which of the following questions can you answer using the map key?

- Which products are produced in Monticello?
- What is the capital of Indiana?
- About how far from the state capital is Bedford?
- Is corn grown east of Muncie?
- Which river forms the southern border of Indiana?

Macmillan/McGraw-Hill

GEO ADVENTURE 124

A National Park

Look at the map of Francis Marion National Forest on page G8 of your social studies textbook. Answer these questions:

- Where is the Francis Marion National Forest located?
- Which wilderness is farthest south?
- How many ranger stations does the national forest have?

Write the answers as sentences on a fact sheet about Francis Marion National Forest. Then add one or more other facts that you can learn from the map.

Macmillan/McGraw-Hill

Time Chart

Use the map of the United States on page R8 of your social studies textbook and the time zone map on page 522 to complete this chart.

City	Time Zone	Time
Reno, Nevada		1:00 P.M.
Madison, Wisconsin		
Memphis, Tennessee		

Copy the chart onto a sheet of paper. Then find each city. Suppose it is 1:00 P.M. in Reno. Figure out the time in each of the other cities and fill it in on the chart.

Macmillan/McGraw-Hill

A Cattle Trail

Turn to the map of Cattle Trails in the West on page 521 of your social studies textbook. Suppose a rancher left San Antonio, Texas, in 1876 and followed the Western Trail north. In which state did the rancher end up? In which city along the way could the rancher have begun a railroad trip?

Macmillan/McGraw-Hill

From Canada to Guatemala

Suppose you have a friend who is traveling on a bus from Ottawa, Canada, to Guatemala City, Guatemala. Use the map of the Western Hemisphere on page R6 of your social studies textbook to describe your friend's trip.

- Which countries will your friend pass through?
- About how many miles will your friend travel before a stop in Monterrey, Mexico?
- About how many miles will your friend still have to travel after the stop in Mexico?

Macmillan/McGraw-Hill

Trails:
True or False?

Turn to the map of trails to the West on page 431 of your social studies textbook. Then copy these sentences:

- **Donner Pass was located along the Oregon Trail.**
- **Whitman's Mission was located near Split Rock.**
- **The Old Spanish Trail led to San Francisco.**
- **Ft. Laramie was located near Soda Springs.**

If a sentence states something true, write *T* next to it. If a sentence is false, write *F* next to it. Rewrite each false sentence to make it true.

Macmillan/McGraw-Hill

United States

Facts from Different Maps

Turn to the political map of the United States on page R8 of your social studies textbook. Find New Mexico. What can you learn about New Mexico by studying the map? On a sheet of paper, write as many facts as you can.

Then turn to the physical map of the United States on page R10. What more can you learn about New Mexico from this map? Add more facts to your list.

Macmillan/McGraw-Hill

GEO ADVENTURE 130

Find the Cities

Use the map of the **Western Hemisphere** on page **R6** of your social studies textbook to find the following cities:

- **Porto Alegre, Brazil**
- **Houston, United States**
- **Nuuk, Greenland**

List the cities on a sheet of paper. Next to each city, write the lines of latitude and longitude that are closest to that city.

Macmillan/McGraw-Hill

United States

Where Are These Cities?

Use the map of the United States on page **R8** of your social studies textbook to find these cities:

- **Sacramento, California**
- **Providence, Rhode Island**
- **Honolulu, Hawaii**

List the cities on a sheet of paper. Next to each city, write the numbers of the lines of latitude and longitude that are closest to that city.

Macmillan/McGraw-Hill

Memphis, Tennessee

Find Memphis, Tennessee, on the map of the United States on page R8 of your social studies textbook. Then answer these questions:

- Which city is closest to Memphis?
- Which city is directly south of Memphis?
- Which city is directly east of Memphis?

Choose from the following cities for the answers:

Charlotte, North Carolina
New Orleans, Louisiana
St. Louis, Missouri

Macmillan/McGraw-Hill

United States

Follow the Directions

Use the map of the United States on page R8 of your social studies textbook to follow these directions:
Start at 40°N latitude, 110°W longitude. Go 30 degrees east. Then go 10 degrees south. Now go 10 degrees west.
In which city are you? What is the latitude and longitude of the city?

Macmillan/McGraw-Hill

GEO
ADVENTURE
134

Mystery
Traveler

Use the maps of the Western Hemisphere on pages R6
and R7 of your social studies textbook to find out
where the mystery traveler went.

The mystery traveler started his trip in Buenos
Aires, Argentina. He followed the Paraná River to a
city in Paraguay. Then he traveled west nearly 1,000
miles across the Andes to a city on the Pacific
Ocean.

On a sheet of paper, write the names of the two cities
the mystery traveler visited.

Macmillan/McGraw-Hill

Mystery Hemisphere

Use the map of the hemispheres on page **G5** of your social studies textbook and the world map on page **R14** to find the mystery hemisphere.

This hemisphere includes the countries of Canada, Uruguay, and Haiti. It does not include Indonesia, Iraq, or Sudan. Which hemisphere is it?

Write the name of the hemisphere on a sheet of paper. Then make up clues for your own mystery hemisphere. Include the names of countries in your clues.

Macmillan/McGraw-Hill

Farthest Apart

Use the map of the Western Hemisphere on page R6 of your social studies textbook to answer this question:
Which cities are farthest apart?
Mexico City, Mexico, and Caracas, Venezuela?
Washington, D.C., and Winnipeg, Canada?
Havana, Cuba, and Bogota, Columbia?
Write the answer on a sheet of paper.

Macmillan/McGraw-Hill

A Northern Border

Turn to the map of the United States on page R8 of your social studies textbook. Use the map scale to answer these questions:

- How long is the northern border of North Carolina?
- Is it longer or shorter than the northern border of Alabama?
- How much longer or shorter is it?

Macmillan/McGraw-Hill

Start in Ohio

Use the map of the United States on page R8 of your social studies textbook to follow these directions:

Start at the state capital of Ohio. Travel southeast for about 450 miles to a city on the coast of Virginia. Then travel about 600 miles to the capital of a state that borders Arkansas to the west. Which three cities have you visited?

Mystery Country

Use the world map on page R14 of your social studies textbook to find the mystery country.

> This country is made up of islands in the Pacific Ocean. It is crossed by 40°N latitude.

Write the name of the mystery country on a sheet of paper. Then make up clues for your own mystery country. Include geographic terms and latitude or longitude in your clues.

Macmillan/McGraw-Hill

Plan a River Trip

Suppose a group of people were planning to take a river trip from Caspar, Wyoming, to Knoxville, Tennessee. Use the maps of the United States on pages R8 and R10 of your social studies textbook to help plan the trip.

- Which rivers might the group follow?
- Which cities might the group pass along the way?
- What kinds of landforms might the group see?

Macmillan/McGraw-Hill

United States

What Am I?

Use the physical map of the United States on page R10 of your social studies textbook to solve this riddle:

I am a body of water directly west of the Wasatch Range and directly east of Mt. Shasta. I am located just north of a desert. What am I?

Write the answer on a sheet of paper. Then use the map to make up a riddle of your own.

Macmillan/McGraw-Hill

United States

Mystery Traveler Code

Turn to the inset map of Europe on page R14 of your social studies textbook. Suppose the mystery traveler gave you this coded message about a trip to Europe:

I'm going to 60°N latitude, 10°E longitude; then to 50°N latitude, 20°E longitude; and finally to 40°N latitude, 30°E longitude.

What countries in Europe does the mystery traveler plan to visit? Write them in order on a sheet of paper.

Macmillan/McGraw-Hill

United States

The Great Basin

Turn to the physical map of the United States on page R10 of your social studies textbook. Then answer these questions about the Great Basin:

- Which mountains are west of the Great Basin?
- Which plateau is north of the Great Basin?
- Which deserts are south of the Great Basin?
- About how wide is the Great Basin?

Write the answers as sentences in a paragraph about the Great Basin.

Macmillan/McGraw-Hill

GEO ADVENTURE 144

Which Is Nearer?

Look at the map of the United States on page **R8** of your social studies textbook. Find **Fort Wayne, Indiana.** Then use the map scale to answer this question:

Which is nearer to **Fort Wayne—Lincoln, Nebraska,** or **Harrisburg, Pennsylvania?**

Write the answer on a sheet of paper. Then write a sentence that tells the distance between **Fort Wayne** and each of the other places.

Macmillan/McGraw-Hill

United States

The Tropic of Cancer

Turn to the map of the world on page R14 of your social studies textbook. Suppose you know someone who plans to follow the Tropic of Cancer around the world. Your friend plans to begin and end his trip in Algeria. He will travel west. Which countries and bodies of water will your friend cross?

Macmillan/McGraw-Hill

GEO
ADVENTURE
146

A Pen Pal
in Europe

Suppose you received a letter from a pen pal in Europe. In the letter your pen pal described her life in a town near the coast of the Baltic Sea. When you began to write back, you discovered that you had lost your pen pal's address.

Use the inset map of Europe on page R14 of your social studies textbook to find countries where your pen pal might live. Make a list of the countries.

Macmillan/McGraw-Hill

Mystery City

Use the map of the United States on page R8 of your social studies textbook and the time zone map on page 522 to find the mystery city. Here are the clues:

When it is 10 A.M. in this state capital, it is 11 A.M. in Washington, D.C. This city is located on the Arkansas River. What is the mystery city?

Write the name of the mystery city. Then write clues for your own mystery city. Use the time zone map to help you write one of your clues.

Macmillan/McGraw-Hill

Facts About Brazil

Turn to the political map of the Western Hemisphere on page **R6** of your social studies textbook. Find **Brazil**. What can you learn about Brazil by studying the map? Write as many facts as you can.

Then look at the physical map of the Western Hemisphere on page **R7**. What more can you learn about Brazil from this map? Add more facts to your list.

Macmillan/McGraw-Hill

Egypt Fact Sheet

Turn to the world map on page R14 of your social studies textbook. Suppose you are making a fact sheet for a group of travelers on their way to Egypt. Write the following information on the fact sheet:

- **Use latitude and longitude to describe the location of Egypt.**
- **Describe a route the travelers might take to get to Egypt from the United States.**
- **Name some of the countries that border Egypt.**

Macmillan/McGraw-Hill

GEO ADVENTURE 150

The World Traveler

Use the map of the world on page R14 of your social studies textbook to follow the path of the world traveler.

> The world traveler started his trip in a country that borders Laos, China, and the Pacific Ocean. Then he traveled north in a straight line until he reached the Arctic Circle. Finally, he followed the Arctic Circle east to 160°W longitude.

In which country is the world traveler now? Which other countries did he visit?

Macmillan/McGraw-Hill

Answer Key

1. The maps should accurately reflect the shape of the state in which students live, include a compass rose, and include a label that shows the correct location of the state capital. The maps should be colored and have an appropriate title.

2. Idaho; to check the accuracy of their clues, you may want to have students read their clues aloud and solve one another's mystery states. At least one clue should contain a direction word and distances in miles.

3. Students should accurately list the states they would cross in order if they were traveling from their state capital to Nashville, Tennessee. Students should also provide the capital of each state on the list.

4. Reno, Nevada: 40°N latitude, 120°W longitude; Springfield, Illinois: 40°N latitude, 90°W longitude; New Orleans, Louisiana: 30°N latitude, 90°W longitude

5. Russia

6. Annapolis, Maryland; Chesapeake Bay

7. Students' paragraphs should include the following information: Alaska is bordered by the Arctic Ocean, the Bering Sea, the Gulf of Alaska, and the Pacific Ocean; Juneau is the capital of Alaska; Mt. McKinley is about 500 miles from the west coast of Alaska.

8. Texas—Corpus Christi, Houston; Louisiana—New Orleans; Mississippi—Biloxi; Alabama—Mobile; Florida—Tampa

9. Maine; to check the accuracy of their clues, you may want to have students read their clues aloud and solve one another's mystery state. At least one clue should contain information about landforms.

10. All three sentences are false and can be rewritten as follows: lines of latitude measure the distance from the equator; lines of longitude are also called meridians; latitude lines extend east and west.

11. Students' charts should include the following information: North America—Northern and Western hemispheres; South America—Southern and Western hemispheres; Europe—Northern and Eastern hemispheres; Africa—Southern, Northern, and Eastern hemispheres; Asia—Southern, Eastern, and Northern hemispheres; Australia—Southern and Eastern hemispheres; Antarctica—Southern, Western, and Eastern hemispheres. Under the *Country* heading on their charts, students should provide the name of a country located on each continent.

12. Peru; to check the accuracy of their clues, you may want to have students read their clues

aloud and solve one another's mystery countries. At least one clue should contain information about latitude and longitude.

13. Students' paragraphs should include the following information: lines of latitude extend from east to west; lines of latitude measure the distance from the equator; lines of longitude extend from north to south; lines of longitude begin and end at the Prime Meridian.

14. Porto Alegre, Brazil; Brazil, Bolivia, Argentina, and Brazil are passed through along the way.

15. Students' answers should accurately reflect the location of their state.

16. North American countries that border the Pacific Ocean and are completely east of 90°W longitude include El Salvador, Honduras, Nicaragua, Costa Rica, and Panama. South American countries that border the Pacific Ocean and are completely south of the equator include Peru and Chile.

17. 60°N latitude, 150° W longitude—Anchorage, Alaska; 60°N latitude, 120°W longitude—Yellowknife, Canada; 30°N latitude, 120°W longitude—Los Angeles, California; 0° latitude, 60°W longitude—Manaus, Brazil

18. Southeast; California, Nevada, Utah, Colorado; Northeast

19. Students' route descriptions may include the following bodies of water: Pacific Ocean, Atlantic Ocean, Indian Ocean, Arctic Ocean.

20. The third sentence is true. The other sentences can be rewritten as follows: the scale on both maps shows miles and kilometers; the scale on map A shows that one inch equals 260 miles, and the scale on map B shows that one inch equals 130 miles.

21. California, Nevada, Utah, Colorado, Kansas/Nebraska (border), Missouri, Illinois, Indiana, Ohio, Pennsylvania, New Jersey

22. Borders an ocean—Georgia; is north of 40°N latitude—North Dakota; is east of 90°W longitude—Georgia

23. Arctic; Aleut; Plains; Basin and Plateau, Southwest, Eastern Woodlands

24. Answers may include: Reno and Carson City, Nevada; Provo, Utah; Denver, Colorado; Springfield, Illinois; Indianapolis, Indiana; Columbus, Ohio; Wheeling, West Virginia; Harrisburg, Pennsylvania; Philadelphia, Pennsylvania; Trenton, New Jersey.

25. Interstate 78. Directions to Johnstown should include: travel west from Harrisburg on Interstate 81; then follow Interstate 76 west to Interstate 70; follow Interstate 70 west; then travel north on route 219 to Johnstown.

26. Colorado River

27. Mountain ranges west of 90°W longitude include: Brooks Range, Alaska Range, Cascade Range, Coast Ranges, Sierra Nevada, Rocky Mountains, Teton Range, and the Wasatch Range. Mountain ranges east of

90°W longitude include: Appalachian Mountains, Allegheny Mountains, Adirondack Mountains, Green Mountains, and White Mountains.

28. Students might write the following: under *northern*—White Mountains, Mt. Washington, Green Mountains, Cape Cod, Hudson River, Long Island, Lake Ontario, Lake Erie, Lake Huron, Lake Michigan, Lake Superior; under *central*—Allegheny Plateau, Appalachian Mountains, Ohio River, Wabash River, Mt. Mitchell, Delaware Bay, Chesapeake Bay, Potomac River; under *southern*—Savannah River, Appalachian Mountains, Chatahoochee River, Alabama River, Mobile Bay, Gulf Coastal Plain, Florida Keys, Straits of Florida, Lake Okeechobee.

29. Montana, Wyoming, Utah, Arizona; to check the accuracy of their clues, you may want to have students read their clues aloud and find one another's mystery states.

30. Students' paragraphs should include the following informa-

tion: the source of the Amazon River is in the Andes Mountains; the mouth of the Amazon River is in Brazil; the Amazon River empties into the Atlantic Ocean.

31. The clues should include the following information: the location of the state, the names of nearby states, and the state capital. To check the accuracy of their clues, you may want to have students read their clues aloud and find one another's mystery states.

32. The first and third sentences can be answered using the map key.

33. shows changes in Earth's surface—elevation, relief; uses shading to show differences in land height—relief; shows land height above sea level—elevation

34. first voyage; San Salvador; 1493; fourth; south; Jamaica; Central America

35. Rio de Janeiro, Brazil, is about 2,000 miles from Lima, Peru. Rio de Janeiro is about 1,000 miles

from Montevideo, Uruguay. Comodoro Rivadavia, Argentina, is about 1,000 miles from Montevideo. You might suggest students use a ruler or map scale strip when determining distances.

36. Brazil, South America

37. United States—Washington, D.C.; Canada—Ottawa; Mexico—Mexico City; Guatemala—Guatemala City; El Salvador—San Salvador; Nicaragua—Managua; Costa Rica—San José; Panama—Panama City

38. Students' paragraphs should include the following information: the equator crosses Ecuador, Colombia, and Brazil; Venezuela, Guyana, Suriname, and French Guiana are entirely north of the equator; Peru, Bolivia, Chile, Argentina, Paraguay, and Uruguay are entirely south of the equator.

39. Guatemala, Honduras, Nicaragua, Costa Rica, Panama

40. Students' paragraphs should include the following informa-

154

tion: the Andes range in found in South America; the Andes extend from north to south; Mt. Aconcagua is 22,834 feet tall.

41. Richmond; Alabama; 300; north

42. The second sentence is true. The other sentences can be rewritten as follows: Mt. Rainier is the fourth tallest mountain in the United States; Mt. Rainier is about 150 miles from Canada.

43. All three sentences are false and can be rewritten as follows: the map shows the 13 colonies in the 1700s; Maine was part of the Massachusetts colony; there were three different groups of colonies in the 1700s.

44. Students' directions should accurately describe how to get from Washington, D.C., to a city that is about 2,000 miles away. Students should list the cities and/or countries they would pass through along the way. You might suggest students use a ruler or map scale strip when determining distances.

45. Students' sentences should include the following informa-

tion: the national capital of Costa Rica is San José (political map); the Saskatchewan River flows from the Rocky Mountains to the Hudson Bay (physical map); Brasília is farther north than Rio de Janeiro (political map).

46. Portland, Oregon

47. On their fact sheets, students should include the following information: the state's latitude and longitude, the other states or bodies of water that border the chosen state, the state's capital, and other cities in the state.

48. Australia, New Caledonia, Chile, Argentina, Paraguay, Brazil, Namibia, Botswana, South Africa, Mozambique, Madagascar

49. The third sentence is true. The other sentences can be rewritten as follows: most of Mexico is south of 30°N latitude; Mexico borders the Pacific Ocean, the Gulf of Mexico, Guatemala, Belize, and the United States.

50. Quebec, Montreal, Port Royal,

or Fort Caroline; Carter or Cabot

51. Begin in Mexico; go east to Algeria; go northeast to Russia.

52. Southern Hemisphere; to check the accuracy of their clues, you may want to have students read their clues aloud and find one another's mystery hemispheres.

53. Students should accurately describe the following route: travel southeast from the tip of Florida to Martinique; from Martinique, southwest to Aruba; from Aruba, northwest to Florida.

54. Kentucky or Tennessee; to check the accuracy of their clues, you may want to have students read their clues aloud and find one another's mystery states.

55. Southeast; about 3,500 miles; the group will pass through Guatemala, Honduras, Nicaragua, Costa Rica, Panama, Colombia, and Brazil.

56. Route 1: from Philadelphia take Interstate 76 west; then take

Macmillan/McGraw-Hill

Interstate 79 north to Erie. Route 2: take state highway 422 north to state highway 322; take state highway 322 west to Interstate 80; take Interstate 80 west to Interstate 79; take Interstate 79 north to Erie.

57. Tallahassee, Florida; Columbia, South Carolina; Pittsburgh, Pennsylvania. To check the accuracy of their directions, you may want to have students listen to and follow one another's directions.

58. shows the location of cities—political map; shows the differences in land height—physical map; has a map scale—political map, physical map

59. Manaus, Brazil: 0° latitude, 60°W longitude; Rosario, Argentina: 30°S latitude, 60°W longitude; Anchorage, Alaska: 60°N latitude, 150°W longitude

60. Students' paragraphs should include the following information: New Hampshire was founded in 1680; Hartford was located in the Connecticut colony; the Massachusetts colony was founded first.

61. Students might indicate that their friend is passing through Guayaquil, Ecuador; Lima, Peru; La Paz, Bolivia; and Tuciman, Argentina. The friend will have traveled about 3,000 miles. You might suggest students use a ruler or map scale strip when determining distances.

62. Peru, Bolivia, Argentina

63. The third sentence is true. The other sentences can be rewritten as follows: the Wasatch Range crosses Utah from north to south; the Great Salt Lake is in northwestern Utah.

64. Pittsburgh, Pennsylvania. Pittsburgh is about 300 miles from New York City, New York. Providence, Rhode Island, is about 150 miles from New York City.

65. Students' paragraphs should include the following information: Trenton was located in the New Jersey colony; Delaware was founded in 1704; New York, New Jersey, and Delaware bordered the Atlantic Ocean.

66. Students' fact sheets should

include the following information: mountains, deserts, and valleys are some of the landforms found in California; the Mojave Desert and the Sonora Desert are found in California; the Pacific Ocean borders the state and the San Joaquin River, the Sacramento River, and the Salton Sea are located within California.

67. is completely east of 90°W longitude—South America; is crossed by the equator—South America; has mountains in the west—North America, South America

68. Argentina; to check the accuracy of their clues, you may want to have students read their clues aloud and find one another's mystery countries.

69. Indonesia; Russia

70. Pecos River; Colorado River; Mojave Desert

71. The third sentence is true. The other sentences can be rewritten as follows: Sweden is north of Poland; the United Kingdom is north of France.

72. Students' sentences might include some of the following: Poland is south of the Baltic Sea; Poland is west of 10°E longitude; Poland is bordered by Germany, Czech Republic, Slovakia, Ukraine, Belarus, Lithuania, and Russia.

73. south; between 90°W longitude and 60°W longitude; Peru, Brazil, Chile

74. Students' paragraphs should include the following information: the Amazon is South America's largest river system; the source of the river is in the Andes mountains; the mouth of the river is located in Brazil; the Amazon River flows through Colombia, Peru, Bolivia, and Brazil.

75. Pittsburgh, Pennsylvania; Charleston, South Carolina; Miami, Florida. To check the accuracy of their clues, you may want to have students read their clues aloud and find the location of one another's mystery travelers.

76. Students should accurately describe the following route: from Brasília, Brazil, travel west about 2,000 miles to Lima, Peru; from Lima, travel southeast about 1,500 miles to Asunción, Paraguay. You might suggest students use a ruler or map scale strip when determining distances.

77. Students' paragraphs should include the following information: the source of the Arkansas River is in Colorado; from Colorado the river flows southeast through Kansas, Oklahoma, and Arkansas, where it meets the Mississippi River; the Arkansas River is about 1,000 miles long.

78. South Carolina; to check the accuracy of their clues, you may want to have students read their clues aloud and find one another's mystery states.

79. dark green; Rochester, Syracuse, Albany, and New York City

80. Canada; to check the accuracy of their clues, you may want to have students read their clues aloud and find one another's mystery countries.

81. Michigan, Wisconsin, Illinois, Missouri, Arkansas, Tennessee, Mississippi, Louisiana

82. Spokane—moderate relief; Seattle—low relief; Olympia—low relief; Yakima—moderate relief

83. Djibouti, Somalia, Kenya, Tanzania, Mozambique, South Africa, Madagascar

84. Eastern Hemisphere; to check the accuracy of their clues, you may want to have students read their clues aloud and find one another's mystery hemispheres.

85. 20°S latitude, 140°E longitude: Australia; 60°N latitude, 140°E longitude: Russia; 60°N latitude, 40°E longitude: Russia; 0° latitude, 40°E longitude: Kenya

86. Spain; to check the accuracy of their clues, you may want to have students read their clues aloud and find one another's mystery countries.

87. Michigan—Lansing; Wisconsin—Madison; Illinois—Springfield; Indiana—Indianapolis; Ohio—Columbus; Pennsylvania—Harrisburg; New York—Albany

88. California, Arizona; to check the accuracy of their clues, you may want to have students read their clues aloud and find one another's mystery states.

89. south; northeast; northwest; northwest

90. Ecuador, Colombia, Brazil; to check the accuracy of their clues, you may want to have students read their clues aloud and find one another's mystery countries.

91. Students' paragraphs should include the following information: Santa Fe is close to both mountains and a river; Santa Fe is close to the Rocky Mountains; Santa Fe is close to the Rio Grande River.

92. Texas, Louisiana, Florida

93. The first, second, and fourth questions can be answered using the map key.

94. Students' fact sheets should include the following information: dairy farms can be found in northeastern, northwestern, and parts of southern Indiana; farms that grow corn are found in the central part of the state; near Ft. Wayne, a person would see dairy farms.

95. 0–500 feet above sea level; higher; students should indicate that they checked the color of the land near Lake Erie and compared it to the elevation scale.

96. Barbados

97. Students' paragraphs should include the following information: the battle at Camden took place in South Carolina; the battle at Saratoga was fought in 1777; battles took place in 1775 in Massachusetts and New York.

98. Boise, Idaho. Boise is about 300 miles from Salt Lake City, Utah. Carson City, Nevada, is about 450 miles away. You might suggest students use a ruler or map scale strip when determining distances.

99. Students' fact sheets should include the following information: the Coast Mountains are located in western Canada; the national capital of Canada is Ottawa; Great Slave Lake and Great Bear Lake are located north of the Saskatchewan River.

100. Canada, the United States, Cuba, Panama, Ecuador, Peru

101. Ohio, Indiana, Illinois, Wisconsin, Michigan; Spain; Great Britain

102. southeast; 600; southwest; 300; northeast; 450

103. The second sentence is true. The other sentences can be rewritten as follows: a time zone is one of the 24 divisions of Earth used for measuring standard time; if it is 4:00 P.M. in New York City, it is 1:00 P.M. in Los Angeles.

104. Northern Hemisphere; to check the accuracy of their clues, you may want to have students read their clues aloud and find one another's mystery hemispheres.

105. Lancaster. Lancaster is about 60 miles from Philadelphia. Pottstown is about 30 miles from Philadelphia. You might suggest students use a ruler or map scale strip when determining distances.

158

106. Students' paragraphs should include the following information: the Lewis and Clark Expedition began and ended in St. Louis; the expedition crossed the Rocky Mountains; the expedition traveled through the Louisiana Purchase area and the Oregon Country.

107. Southwest; about 600 miles. After Wichita, the friend might visit Topeka, Kansas, or Tulsa, Oklahoma.

108. Students should accurately describe the following route: from Gibraltar travel east to the southeastern tip of Sicily; from Sicily travel southeast to Crete.

109. Argentina, Chile, Peru, Brazil, Colombia, Venezuela, Caribbean Sea, Dominican Republic, Atlantic Ocean, United States, Canada, Baffin Bay, Greenland, Canada

110. Bismarck, North Dakota

111. Students' responses and explanations should reflect their understanding that they add an hour for each time zone east of where they are and subtract an hour for each time zone west of where they are.

112. Santiago, Chile: south of 30°S latitude and west of 60°W longitude; Buenos Aires, Argentina: south of 30°S latitude and east of 60°W longitude; Georgetown, Guyana: north of 0° latitude (equator) and east of 60°W longitude

113. Oregon Trail; Ft. Bridger; Independence Rock, Red Buttes, Split Rock, South Pass

114. Virginia, Tennessee, Mississippi, Arkansas; Texas

115. The first and third sentences are true. The other sentence can be rewritten as follows: the elevation map shows the height above sea level of the Columbia Plateau.

116. Northern Pacific Railroad; the family traveled on the Atchinson, Topeka, and Santa Fe Railroad, then changed to the Atlantic and Pacific Railroad, which brought them to Los Angeles.

117. is in the Central Time Zone—Wisconsin, Arkansas; is crossed by 90°W latitude—Wisconsin, Arkansas; is north of 40°N latitude—Wisconsin

118. 40°N latitude, 100°W longitude: United States; 40°N latitude, 140°E longitude: Japan; 20°S latitude, 20°E longitude: Namibia; 0° latitude, 20°E longitude: Congo

119. From Denver the friend would travel about 450 miles through Colorado and Wyoming to Pocatello, Idaho. She would travel in the Mountain Time Zone. From Pocatello the friend would travel about 600 miles through Idaho, Oregon, and Washington to Seattle, Washington. She would travel in the Mountain and Pacific time zones.

120. Erie; Johnstown

121. La Paz, Bolivia, to Santiago, Chile. The distance from La Paz to Santiago is about 1,000 miles, and the distance from Mexico City, Mexico, to New York City, New York is about 2,000 miles. You might suggest students use a ruler or map scale strip when determining distances.

United States•Answer Key   Macmillan/McGraw-Hill

122. Utah, Texas, Pennsylvania

123. The first, second, and fourth sentences can be answered using the map key.

124. Students' fact sheets should include the following information: the Francis Marion National Forest is located in eastern South Carolina; the Wambaw Swamp Wilderness is farthest south; the national forest has two ranger stations.

125. Reno, Nevada—Pacific Time Zone; Madison, Wisconsin—Central Time Zone, 3 P.M.; Memphis, Tennessee—Central Time Zone, 3 P.M.

126. Nebraska; Dodge City, Kansas

127. United States, Mexico, Guatemala; about 2,000 miles; about 1,000 miles

128. All of the sentences are false and can be rewritten as follows: Donner Pass was located along the California Trail; Whitman's Mission was located near Ft. Walla Walla; the Old Spanish Trail led to Los Angeles; Ft. Laramie was located near Castle Rock and Chimney Rock.

129. Facts learned from the political map might include some of the following: New Mexico borders Arizona, Colorado, and Texas; Santa Fe is the capital of New Mexico; Albuquerque is located along the Rio Grande. Facts learned from the physical map might include some of the following: the Pecos River flows from north to south in New Mexico; Wheeler Peak is 13,065 feet high; much of New Mexico is mountainous.

130. Porto Alegre, Brazil: 30°S latitude, 60°W longitude; Houston, Texas: 30°N latitude, 90°W longitude; Nuuk, Greenland: 60°N latitude, 60°W longitude

131. Sacramento, California: 40°N latitude, 120°W longitude; Providence, Rhode Island: 40°N latitude, 70°W longitude; Honolulu, Hawaii: 20°N latitude, 160°W longitude

132. St. Louis, Missouri; New Orleans, Louisiana; Charlotte, North Carolina

133. New Orleans, Louisiana; 30°N latitude, 90°W longitude

134. Asunción, Paraguay; Antofagasta, Chile

135. Western Hemisphere; to check the accuracy of their clues, you may want to have students read their clues aloud and find one another's mystery hemispheres.

136. Mexico City, Mexico, and Caracas, Venezuela

137. About 300 miles long; longer; 150 miles

138. Columbus, Ohio; Norfolk, Virginia; Nashville, Tennessee

139. Japan; to check the accuracy of their clues, you may want to have students read their clues aloud and find one another's mystery countries.

140. Rivers that the group might follow include: Platte River, Missouri River, Mississippi River, Tennessee River. Cities the group might pass include: Omaha, Nebraska; Kansas City, Kansas; Kansas City, Missouri; Jefferson City, Missouri; St.

160

Louis, Missouri. Landforms the group might see include plains and hills.

141. Great Salt Lake; to check the accuracy of their clues, you may want to have students read their clues aloud and solve one another's riddles.

142. Norway, Poland, Turkey

143. Students' paragraphs should include the following information: the Sierra Nevada, Cascade Range, Coast Ranges, Brooks Range, and Alaska Range are west of the Great Basin; the Columbia Plateau is north of the Great Basin; the Mojave and Sonora deserts are south of the Great Basin; the Great Basin is about 450 miles wide.

144. Harrisburg, Pennsylvania. Harrisburg is about 450 miles from Fort Wayne, Indiana, and Lincoln, Nebraska, is about 600 miles from Fort Wayne. You might suggest students use a ruler or map scale strip when determining distances.

145. Algeria, Mali, Mauritania, Morocco, Atlantic Ocean, Cuba, Gulf of Mexico, Mexico, Pacific Ocean, Taiwan, China, Myanmar, India, Bangladesh, India, Pakistan, Oman, United Arab Emirates, Saudi Arabia, Egypt, Libya, Algeria

146. Denmark, Germany, Poland, Russia, Lithuania, Latvia, Estonia, Finland, Sweden

147. Little Rock, Arkansas; to check the accuracy of their clues, you may want to have students read their clues aloud and find one another's mystery cities.

148. Facts learned from the political map might include some of the following: Brazil is bordered by Uruguay, Argentina, Paraguay, Bolivia, Peru, Colombia, Venezuela, Guyana, Suriname, and French Guiana; the capital of Brazil is Brasília; Porto Alegre and Rio de Janeiro are cities in Brazil that are located near the Atlantic Ocean. Facts learned from the physical map might include some of the following: the Amazon River flows in northern Brazil; the Mato Grosso Plateau is located in western Brazil; the Brazilian Highlands are found near the coast of the Atlantic Ocean.

149. Students' fact sheets should include the following information: Egypt is located between 20°N latitude and 40°N latitude, and 20°E longitude and 40°E longitude; from the United States, travelers might cross the Atlantic Ocean, then the countries of Morocco, Algeria, and Libya to get to Egypt; countries that border Egypt include Libya, Sudan, and Israel.

150. United States; Vietnam, Russia

Macmillan/McGraw-Hill